The Figure of a Man Being Swallowed by a Fish

PHOENIX POETS

JOSHUA WEINER

The Figure of a Man
Being Swallowed by a Fish

THE UNIVERSITY OF CHICAGO PRESS

Chicago & London

JOSHUA WEINER is professor of English at the University of Maryland. He is the author of *The World's Room* and *From the Book of Giants* and the editor of *At the Barriers: On the Poetry of Thom Gunn*, all published by the University of Chicago Press. He lives in Washington, DC.

The University of Chicago Press, Chicago 60637
The University of Chicago Press, Ltd., London
© 2013 by The University of Chicago
All rights reserved. Published 2013.
Printed in the United States of America
22 21 20 19 18 17 16 15 14 13   1 2 3 4 5

ISBN-13: 978-0-226-01701-3 (paper)
ISBN-13: 978-0-226-01715-0 (e-book)

Library of Congress Cataloging-in-Publication Data
Weiner, Joshua.
The figure of a man being swallowed by a fish / Joshua Weiner.
pages. cm.
Includes bibliographical references.
ISBN: 978-0-226-01701-3 (pbk. : alk. paper)
ISBN: 978-0-226-01715-0 (e-book)
I. Title.
PS3573.E3937F354 2013
811'.54—dc23   2012023408

⊚ This paper meets the requirements of ANSI/NISO Z39.48-1992 (Permanence of Paper).

What meanest thou, O sleeper?

Jonah 1:5–6

CONTENTS

ACKNOWLEDGMENTS

Thanks to the editors of the following journals, where some of these poems were first published:

B O D Y: "Things To Do While You're Here"
Harvard Review: "Cyclops"
Literary Imagination: "Rock Creek"
The Literary Review: "Rock Creek (II)"
The New Republic: "Hikmet: Çankiri Prison, 1938"
New York Review of Books: "First Walk after Cancer"
Ploughshares: "'The Figure of a Man Being Swallowed by a Fish'"
Southwest Review: "The Winter's Tale"
TriQuarterly: "Florida: Schoolboy on Break"

Thanks to the Banff Centre, Fine Arts Work Center in Provincetown, Hawthornden Castle, Vermont Studio Center & ALSCW, and the University of Maryland for time and material support.

One

ROCK CREEK (II)

Cutting a way through stone
to see what's there, not
how things appear, earth-blood,
without style, never
at rest, what settles in it
read on the surface
ripples meandering
forward eddying back
swirling turbid intricate plaits of
water from the bottom rising
turning upside down
striking bank before
returning to stream center
original current
indifferent to the play of light
crystalline ideal forms
a static lie, rather
as Leonardo saw
a motion resembling hair
"one must take five days
to place water in a picture"
while a splash erupts
into corona, its rim
breaking into spills
of droplets like the secret
structure of rainfall

scalloped edges of water
joining water in common
coil spawning vortices
streamlines detaching
as they hit fluorescent storm-swept
traffic cones glowing
half-submerged
shedding eddies
rushing faster by
tightening gorge
squeezed
self-amplifying
transmission as one
flow drives another
motion altering force
driving that motion
like Coltrane stretching
tight vibrato
phrases
incremental shifts
of pitch & tone
the place it's going
unknown excited
viscous harmonies
continuously born/
devoured, cascades
of smaller scales
circulating airstreams
"the unregarded river of our life"
an overflow of "meanings
with no speech"

undirected
as prisoners of
Guantánamo
flooding cells in protest
each drinking
eighteen bottles of water
in an hour. And the breath,
preaches one man
having heard it from his father,
"the breath moved
upon the face of the waters,"
while another speaks
ex-con/activist, wry
observer at the crossroads,
how "the system is hustling
backward."

———

Not a river of history
like the Patawmack—
big muddy highway
Washington dreamed
would connect the capital
to a bountiful interior
budging west, make him rich
and keep the money moving
"to bind all parts together
by one indissoluble band"—
the founding's first boondoggle
"designated by law for the seat of Empire"—
No, Rock Creek's histories

converge as branches
braiding like scoubidou
a single spiral knotting
that children weave to hold their keys
it makes just one boundary of the verdant valley
where L'Enfant walked in great coat
surveying space
so every homestead of the nation
would feel the influence of its streets
radiating outward
and slaves hew trees to open them
metabolize sardines and salt pork
to pry up stumps, haul, and cut sandstone
for buildings housing classical
moral sentiments that shan't
stop the flow of profits.
                              Neither Rome, nor home
Rock Creek is a passage
                              where Whitman wanders
after dispensing fruit syrups—
"good and strong, but innocent"—
mixed with ice water
to young men missing limbs,
thirsty, coated with murk & sweat
in the Patent Office hospital.

———

The 9:30 Club is not named for a time
but a place it used to be, 930 F Street,
now in a building on V, once broadcasting
1120 on your radio. Inside, my son plays drums

in a band with other nine-year-olds
trying to rock the judge's panel, 11 AM, a Saturday.
And the parents are pumped, pulling for their kids
on stage, a discrete loud screening
of their own projections. Is it strange
to hear children play their parents' music,
the history of styles like scarves claimed
from an old trunk that's never put away. . . .
"They lend me a problem with the language,"
Fugazi, twenty-five years ago, "But still /
I was caught with my hand in the till."
Up the street at Howard
Don Byrd's Blackbyrds'
"Walking in Rhythm" hit big,
but it's "Rock Creek"—"Doin' it in the park /
Doin' it after dark"—that laid down a track in '75
for Eric B. & Rakim, Big Daddy Kane,
Grandmaster Flash, Massive Attack,
the gold spinning still, the chorus
floating with Jay Jones' flute
on a current sampled
by a cloud precipitating
the next good sound.

———

Oak, tulip poplar, beech & laurel
holly, dogwood on the hills,
sycamore, red maple, wet,
tolerant, all along the floodplain
through steep ravines, gentle
sloping hills, grassy meadows

and the stretch of rapids
south of Military Road,
the Secession War captured in a street sign
now as frenzied commuter route
where 20,000 years ago
nomads sharpened fluted points
for caribou, elk, moose,
black bear, mastodon & mammoth;
the spring-fed tributaries
feeding into open stream
are sewer lines underground,
silt & sand choke off
the creek mouth at Whitehurst Freeway
where ships ran up to P Street
from Potomac's crowd of masts;
and grist mills—Lyons, Deakins,
Parrott, Peirce, Columbian—all
ran out of time to grind; and Benjamin Stoddert—
milliner, first secretary of the navy,
who bought up land to create the capital—
now names the kiddie soccer team,
an elementary school: in limbo,
neither remembered nor forgotten.

———

If Rock Creek is a passage
what will I find there
in its leaves & pages, legible
by moonlight, having passed by
the White House of future poems,
its sentries at the gates, silent,

pacing in blue overcoats, stopping you
not at all, but eyeing you with sharp eyes
whichever way you move—
Whichever way
                              you move, with me now
from hospital to hospice of the creek,
the pallid face of wounded
light your way; and in the air,
the moisture on the lip of the secesh boy,
his fine large frame, patient
mute survivor of the butcher's shambles,
his arm tossed on the departing amputation cart. . . .
Little he knew, poor death-stricken boy,
the heart of the stranger that hover'd near,
talked to him a little, but not much,
moved closer, held his hand,
and moves now in creek shadows,
searching, fluid & firm . . .

                    —

There's the cavalry camp on the hill
& fixed pitch droning
of an Ozark juice harp, its tart
plucked notes opening melodic
overtones bring to mind
parted teeth & metal tongue
vibrating freely, whiskey-wet
mouth resonator!
                              So refreshing,
these hardy, bright, intuitive
American young men; experienced

with all their youth, their vocal play
moves one more
than books.
           Bloody pieces
of muslin fill buckets by
one who follows me, I carry him
wherever I go, his great dark eyes
with a glaze already upon them
the choking faint but audible
in his throat; and the surgeon who
left him, without prospect, to death
he must yield the field, and forget.
And the population of the army
bedded in the makeshift wards
is more numerous than the whole
of Washington; some thirty or forty
such collections, each holding
seventy thousand men, I use them
as landmarks in my rambling outside
the district of wounds, sickness, & death.

—

What will I find there, then,
if Rock Creek is a passage,
the crown of haze
around the moon
like stardust inked around
the gunner's nipple.
                Something
veil'd, abstracted, dark
columns moving through the night

and I stand, unobserv'd in the darkness
and watch them long, my own
longing
          charged with the intimacies
of the ward. But when I join
the soldiers along the creek
or defending the capital behind earthworks
acres of felled trees, hewn branch barriers
with sharpened points, they invite me
to declaim poetical pieces,
read the Bible, and we play an amusing game
called the game of twenty questions.

——

If Rock Creek is a passage
what will I find there
below terraced bluffs
overcasting intemperate
fall freshet conveying
fragmented stone tools of the Algonquin
quartzite, slate, jasper, flint,
past Teddy Roosevelt
pounding down a routine
rough cross-country jaunt
overtaking Quincy Adams
"listening to the singing of a thousand birds"
along beds of shallow
estuary out to sea. . . .
In the mind's perpetual
playback, the boys & I
stand a stone's throw from Peirce Mill

performing tashlikh on Rosh Hashanah,
"casting off" our sins
in the body of breadcrumbs
tossed into the stream—
we try to track them
out of sight, alert to
blueback herring plucking some down,
with no lids their eyes are always open,
like God they do not sleep,
they do not avoid the net,
"nothing is exhausted if it returns to itself"
as rich veins run
without celestial fallings from cloud
nor collected lake dropping down,
so it is *living water*, exploiting
its own nature.

———

To be preserved in the seed that never falls nor changes. A dream.
Whereas, from the surface of silence, under the pressure of river
wonder that moves through the green heights, the old woman in
the parking lot of Giant grabbed me by the arm on my way to the
car, four bags of ice in hand for the school football team. A warm
September Saturday, the bags begin to drip. What does she want?
She can't open the back hatch of her van, the electronic key, it's not
hers, it's borrowed, she's just been evicted. Her muddy brown eyes
are enormous. I can see the shadowy mounds of domestic debris in
the beat up oatmeal-colored van. Does she need to buy something?
Some food? No, she has recycling to drop off, she has to drop off
her recycling, how do you open the back? The ice is dripping, the
cubes are fusing in their melting. Her fragility & panic gripping me,

I lay the bags down on the warm tarmac and show her how the key
works. She takes the key and tries to open the door. She can't do it.
I show her again how the key works, you just press it there, hold it.
The hatch opens, and I lift it up.

She'll never be able to reach that high to close it herself. She takes
the key and practices opening the doors and locking them while I
grab some empty bottles to carry to the bins—*Not those!* she yells
at me, *those stay!* Okay, which, these? *No, not those!* Okay, these?
No, no, no, no! I just want to finish, to help her and go. Where is she
driving to? She stares at me. From the plastic bags, a stream of ice-
melt is running along the contours & cracks of the blacktop, pick-
ing up grains of dust and carrying them away. . . .

——

A passage, and what I find there—
swifter moving water
increased by rain.
Coarse-toothed box-elder leaves
vessels in the current
passing through reflections
ruffling on the surface
some submerged like thoughts
you hardly know you're thinking
they're moving too, and others
still dropping have yet
to reach the boundary.
                    What did
the furniture maker find there
between oak & poplar
shading the western ridge?

As a boy, he'd go out looking
for coon's bones, bones of the vole,
mouse, rat; feathers
of gnatcatcher, bunting, bobolink, jay.
"We're like animals," he'd think,
"we come and go; and you never know
what you're going to find."
On his walk that May 22, 2002,
he could hear passing cars
along Broad Branch in the distance;
that's where he found the bones
of the Bureau of Prisons intern,
Chandra Ann Levy
of the San Joaquin Valley,
the scandal of her disappearance
forgotten after 9/11. Soon
maps of Rock Creek replaced
maps of Afghanistan on TV
and cadaver dogs searched
wild flower & trout lily,
butterfly weed & spice bush understory
and they found more bones than expected
near Grove 17.
              Ingmar Adalid Guandique,
the immigrant from El Salvador,
grew up in a hamlet
outside San Miguel, in a family
of poor farmers of cotton, rice, & corn.
He worked construction in DC
and his girlfriend waited tables
at Cactus Cantina, where we go sometimes

to escape the luxury of our own kitchen.
When he killed her, *if he killed her*,
the one he didn't know, did the sound
of water cascading over boulders and merging
with traffic noise echoing through the ravine
join sound of the Rio Grande
he swam across to Texas,
drops of river finding a way
into the canal of his open ear?
Was it the hex
the mother of his boy put on him
when child support dried up?
Or was it the culminating course of
killings that started with his father,
pressed into joining leftist guerillas
fighting military junta death squads
backed by Reagan in the 80s,
his father one of 75,000 killed in civil war,
dumped on a country road that flowed
backward to the proxy wars
of *kholodnaya voyna?* "The vision
of all that happened with my daughter
being out there in Rock Creek,"
said Susan Levy to a reporter,
"the skeletal remains. It is there still
in my mind." Among cinnamon fern & wood roach
I too and others see them
not far from where I find myself
walking along the creek, and the adobe house
Guandique grew up in, with a roof
of tree branches, an open cooking pit

in the middle of a dirt floor, mixing spores & fungus
outside ancient Piscataway wigwam,
& the beatings his mother gave him,
& the man who married her,
not his father, who lay unburied on the road
(*and who found his bones?*) whether or not
his son is guilty, far from the deep loud long
accusing rumbling roar I hear
of zoo lions at sunset
from across Duke Ellington Bridge.

———

If Rock Creek is a passage
what will I find there now
if not a poem called "Rock Creek"
I wrote a few years ago
"past the comfort of known limit"—
but too limited, the poem,
I came to think,
like the flow on
Slash Run, long buried
or the strong stream head
Peirce needed to turn the mill wheel.
"My river is mine own and I have made it
for myself," as "the water that I touch
is the last of what has passed
& the first of that which comes,
so with the present."
                            But when
sycamore roots
siphon into itself

the creek it sits alongside of
and a new flow inside the tree
synthesizes time
an over branching crown
sends down seeds in early spring
dispersed by wind & water,
so too the fruit hangs waiting
on a long stalk through the winter.
Counterrotating chopper blades
fight torque in the air above
as turbulence in the stream
coils clockwise & counterclockwise
whirlpools speeding up around the spindle
downstream unspooling
                      the forces of its
influence a number without dimension.
And it's not enough to just observe
"varieties of incandescence"
efforts of a "common sound"
caught like chatter of common warbler
in practiced improvising form.
Thirty-three miles it meanders, heavy
metals, phosphorus, chlorides, fertilizer,
sad limp balloons, used condoms & needles,
dead animals, bottles & cans.
The pastoral cannot contain them, toxic
banalities emerging even from sickness, war, & death,
a kind of plankton in the current
of storm overflow events.
                      And when my boys
carefully step from stone

to stone in crossing, they must not slip
which makes the slipping much more fun
& a fact without recourse
happening and always about to happen,
until they're wading chest-high
happy as otters.
                But in their mother's mind
she's tracking the time they're in there,
and tomorrow, in a basement corner,
I'll find the wet clothes rank,
petroleum runoff, ethers, esters,
monocyclic aromatics . . .

———

But Rock Creek is still a passage
and I go, it's not Innisfree,
though you'll find a log cabin there,
the "Poet of the Sierras" built it,
"The Kit Carson of Poetry"
when he moved to Washington, DC.
Who remembers his poem, "Columbus" (1892),
once memorized across the land
by children compelled in school?

Then pale and worn, he kept his deck,
    And peered through darkness. Ah, that night
Of all dark nights! And then a speck—
    A light! A light! A light! A light!
It grew, a starlight flag unfurled!
    It grew to be Time's burst of dawn.
He gained a world; he gave that world
    It's greatest lesson: "On! Sail on!"

He braided rhyme like a Christmas wreath
   With an ear that heard "Goethe" rhyme with "teeth."
Go Eath, old man, settle old frontiers
   To occupy my middle years!

———

If Rock Creek is a passage
what will I find there
young men obeying the events
& occasions about them, unaware
of their own nature. The sick
poor wrecks & phantoms
coming along Seventh Street,
passing slowly up
from the steamboat wharf with loads.
And amid the woods, mud huts & mule teams,
heaps of forage, hay, horse carcass,
& old flag shot through with fragments,
silk stained, fringed as with the sword,
& nearby the soldiers sleeping,
whoe'r can write the story?
                 Quite often
they arrive at the rate of a thousand a day,
and every day in the district papers
they print the hospital directories.
Often at Walter Reed I go distributing
myself & the contents of my pockets
good jelly, spiced fruits, pickle,
tobacco, undershirts, drawers, stockings, writing paper,
envelopes, pencils, licorice,
raspberry vinegar, pipe, horehound candy,
a comb, a toothpick.

Lots of them have grown
to expect as I leave at night
that we should kiss each other—
sometimes quite a number. I know
what is in their hearts—
always waiting—
though they may be unconscious of it themselves,
the soldiers know how to love, too,
when once they have the right person
and the right love offered them.
You see how
              I am running off into the clouds. . . .

Exiting, I pass
the old finishing school for young ladies
now the Forest Glen, dead pastoral
with its Japanese pagoda & Dutch windmill
stirring the evening air, the main PX store,
the Robin Hood Deli, where I pick up
some vagabond literature, the Center's
Hero Handbook lost under piles of
The Rock Creek Free Press tabloid,
"Does the United States maintain
a plan for the continuity of government
through suspension of the Constitution?"
"Did the CIA Kill Jimi Hendrix?"
And what about the "stagnant pools of money"
the states keep from the national economy?
"Reassure your child
that the family member injured
is still the same person

even though he or she may look different.
Use accurate language
when describing the family member's injury.
If you say the loved one lost a limb
the child may think it was simply misplaced.
Teach your child
the vocabulary of the injury. Knowing words
such as 'prosthesis,' 'rehabilitation,' and 'physical therapy'
can take out the mystery
and help your child feel
more in control. *Give your child something*
to bring. Common reactions include
crying, clinging, searching,
regression to earlier behaviors,
repetitive play or talk,
fighting, tantrums, outbursts, withdrawal,
regression to earlier behaviors,
sleep difficulty, acting as if
the person is not injured, increased
fear, anger, bullying, denial,
self-blame, fluctuating moods,
fear of separation or being alone,
headaches, stomachaches, difficulty concentrating at school.
While powerless
to protect military children from difficult life experiences
there are ways we can work together
to make transformations
as positive as possible.
Are you experienced /
Have you ever been
experienced? Many injured experience

nightmares, unwanted
thoughts, impatience, flashbacks,
irritability, avoidance, numbness,
guilt, shame, grief, depression, lack of trust,
negative self-image and view of the world
and increased arousal is also a common response.
Remember, go slowly,
don't try to make up for lost time."

———

Another passage at Rock Creek I didn't expect to find floated to
me in the form of pages from the notebook of a man I had met and
only recently befriended. The pages contained some poems; and,
although he invited any comments, in truth the work was not pre-
sented for my opinion, but as gesture of fellowship. *What made*
me turn to him at dinner to offer my pathetic weak notions?—To call
them insights would be unbearably pompous, and whoever had the
misfortune of sitting near such mental litter would have thought as
much. John didn't understand what I was trying to convey, nor, it
was clear from the pained look on his face, why I was trying to con-
vey it. I had trespassed onto his poems, to display some gaudy pre-
tentious wares I called *thoughts.* I had stirred up the mud below the
clear current that carried us in a singular element.

———

Rock Creek is a passage
it is not a law, one follows it
before understanding. You follow it
like your parents' music
till the good sound is a new
good sound

changed into something you make yours.
There is a place in the creek
where you might step into the same water twice
where the down streaming vortex opens
and makes its way
back up along the bank
turning at a concave boulder
where turning water wore it away,
and that streamline turning
& moving downstream
then veers toward the bank
and makes its way back up.
If the sun's out, it's hard to see,
it's clearer when it's cloudy,
there's less reflected light.

Spring shad hang in the slacks
their launch
                    over the baffles
delayed
          to breathe more

before they fire
                    up the ladder of origin
to spawn in pools they dreamed of
in the tides of larger waters.

───

When you step into the creek
you're still outside it; therefore,
outside of it, you feel the water

moving through you. The logic
may seem false, but the sudden
chill will make you sneeze.
And what you find there
                    in the passage
as the sun goes down
is the shadow of the shagbark
lengthening on the water
until the longer coursing shadow
drinks it up
                    to carry it away
as if it were a kind of rain
like words that continue the silence
undirected by any motive
it mixes with the dust
and on the bodies of animals
enters the colder stream.

Two

"THE FIGURE OF A MAN BEING SWALLOWED BY A FISH"

is not a man being swallowed by a fish
with eyes like eight-point throwing stars
it's a man being swallowed by a war
a man being taken into the mouth of a woman
or being swallowed by his work

it's a man traveling far inside a book
a man being swallowed up in smoke
he swallows the smoke, that blends around him like a thought
it's a man being swallowed by a sound
he shapes it so he lives inside a song

of a man being swallowed by his kin, his skin
a man being swallowed by the State
(Leviathan in 1948)
It's a man being swallowed by another man
literally, eaten as a pathway to god

it's a man being swallowed by a sight
he cannot reach, cannot touch, cannot trace

it's a man who won't recognize his face
who can't fit the parts, or find the place

it's a man in triumph over death
who laughs and beats the dust from his clothes
a man tasting dust inside the laugh

it's a man who listens to the clock
a man with nothing to exchange
a rude man, his twin he leaves behind
it's a man who wants to be a bride

a man being swallowed by his fault
with something old to show and new to hide

it's a man who tries to haul the rope
a man who stooping can't provide
a man who can't forget his name

it's a man who doesn't know his worth
it's a man being swallowed by his wrath

his youth, yield, luck, the law, his fear, the fog, his fame

it's a man being swallowed by a coat
his father's coat, he smells of the fit
a man being swallowed by his vows
it's a man softly squeezing for the vein
he never finds it, he's minding the road

it's a man being swallowed by a room
in which he finds a man being swallowed by a fish
it's a man who thinks what's in a man
who exits into night at closing time
the figure of a man being swallowed by a fish.

FLORIDA: SCHOOLBOY ON BREAK

Eager to make a catch, any catch he can,
he grips the rod and sets eye on the bobber;
imagining the strike, he wants to reel it in
to see what's lurking in the water.

The intracoastal avenue is calm
until bridge jaws open to let a tall mast pass;
he loves the clap of wake on concrete wall,
he hates the shrimp blood on his hand. Time

swells, he's an empty raft, God's floater.
But then the rod bends, he pulls, reels, electrically alive,
and there's joy in blood, I smell it in his voice,
the puffer fish ballooning now so fast

it's like a ball dolphins nip for play, to get a toxin high,
and it blinks, unique in air, common and afraid.

FIRST WALK AFTER CANCER

New ugly house (too big) with girl on porch
cradling lacrosse stick; a Spanish lady, lost?
speaking Spanish to Bluetooth in her ear;
tied rods of rebar webbing a bridge under repair;

dude in red shorts, running—Hey, it's not that warm!
no red wheelbarrow; white chick
of seductive frame; ruined snow,
wet street; sun meeting my face

like a brother in a hospital room;
laborers from China in hard hats and uniforms
traversing embassy foundation, just a giant hole;
Israeli grounds next door, cordoned off with cable,

cameras at all corners; cops in car across
the street, 7-11 coffee cooling on the hood;
lost glove in bare tree; blue jay; my favorite shoes:
green lights everywhere, seen, if not understood.

THINGS TO DO WHILE YOU'RE HERE

I was at Disney World, by myself. How long had I been there? Surrounded, but without companion. The rides did not look fun. When I ran into a Disney character on the street I felt uneasy. There's Pluto, mute, unnaturally upright and intrepid on his two hind feet, a wide happy dog smile cut into the snout; from tip of black nose bulb to saucer-size black pupil looked the length of a torso. Could I make out the sweating human body inside the heavy plush construction?—Hardly a costume, the cramping box of the "little ease." . . . And if I had a knife? Would I wrestle him down and liberate the body from its gainful employment?

I wandered aimlessly, from Frontierland to Tomorrowland to Liberty Square, eating Disney food and looking for a chair, away from the crowd, where I could sit and read the book I was carrying. I found myself again in a busy picnic area. Its dishevelment settled my nerves. I found an open bench, sat down, and opened the book on the long wooden table. Soon I was lost in a sentence, a cadence. My physical surroundings became a faint background to my book. The world slowed down. I was content, without worry. The sun was making the pages warm and crinkly, old pages. My elbows on the wood were not unpleasantly hot. Even as the wood got hotter, it was not unpleasant. But the brightness was making me dizzy.

Something made me look up. Dogs were surrounding me in a semicircle, six of them. With eye contact, the six dogs began a low growling. Their heads lowered, napes bristling; coarse-haired, scrawny. I could count their ribs. They were baring their teeth, their ulcerated gums. Something was wrong with them. Parts of their bodies had been shaved. Patches of scaly grey skin showed stitches. Had they been subjected to experiments? With a step toward me the circle was tightening. *Can someone please help me? These dogs are going to hurt me.* I was standing up, speaking out loud. *Can someone please help me please?* The sun was blinding in the blue sky, it was burning my neck. No one paid attention, they were all outside the circle of dogs. But here's my friend Jonathan. Inside the closing circle. When did he appear? The circle was slowly closing. Had he been there all along? In a calm voice he was explaining something. His voice had a quiet authority, a softness and firmness I could hear before I made out the words he was saying. *The problem is time. The problem is you can't stop it.* A subtle shadow passed over his face. The skin was drawn back from his mouth a little. He was slowly but visibly aging as he spoke. Now he looked younger, now older. Age ebbed in his face like tidal water. *It's not a special problem. It's a problem for everyone.* He was studying the dogs. *But you can shape it.* He turned from the dogs to the spires of the Magic Kingdom, its color and clamor. Vanilla and frying oil fragranced the air, mixing with the smell of hot garbage. He turned back to the closing circle of dogs. *This is your nightmare, but you can do something with it.* And for what seemed a long time I chose not to wake up.

WINTER COMMUTE

Dear friend, asleep
   upright in a seat
when I boarded the train
   goat-stepping over
your legs outstretched
   why didn't I wake you
but instead watched
   you sleep, watched over
you two seats away
   but, no, merely
watched, still
   life, face
no longer fresh
   but a peach
sweet even
   as skin loosens from
flesh flesh
   from pit those little
wrinkles you can make
   with a thumb press
kissing the outer
   orbit of your eyes
the longer lines
   charted
down crescent cheeks
   your jaw relaxed

lips parted neat
	compact woman's
body buttoned up
	in business darks
foggy gray
	starched contrasts
at neckline & cuff
	what reprieve here
shuttling underground
	before the courted
client you must meet
	is met you're floating
somewhere where
	the car's cold rays
can't reach, absorbed in
	other versions, in-
version of a life
	as when we watch
children sleep
	so far from us
we don't dare wake them
	in the uncontrollable
uncontrolled
	are you back there now
in your own deep new
	episode without
pillow or comforter or
	parent standing over
you at night but for
	a few minutes at peace

with stolen rest
    hurtling motionless
forgive me for not
    sitting down beside you
placing a hand
    softly on your tailored
arm to call you back
    when all I could have
offered: weak pleasantries
    phatic discharging
of routines impositions
    variegated surfaces
of elected obligations
    what does one
owe another
    in common
what comfort what
    welcome release
rehearsed in
    the dark, dark clad
friend, foe,
    Proserpina or Pluto
shape-shifting
    roles all play
haphazardly
    in false fundament
decked out in
    eye-open finery
embroidered so
    elaborately it's ripped

right off our backs.
   That afternoon
when my stop came
   I left you suspended
in your frail respite
   and haven't seen you since.

THE WINTER'S TALE

It's about jealousy without cause,
    a king who thinks his queen deceives him;
or some truth that hides inside
    a seeming, how it glisters
through rust, how dreams are toys, authority
    a stubborn bear. It's about a man
rebelling against himself, lost in silent
    judgment after condemning innocents.
Then when the dead return to life,
    it's a comedy: everyone marries and remarries,
natural order restored, and the salve of
    second chances curing injury of tongue.
Art mocks us, so we applaud
    such unity in the proofs.

But watching you playing the Sicilian prince,
    still just a boy
who exits in the second act, dies offstage,
    and won't come back to life (because it's not
written that way). . . . Yes, poignant enough, and
    with the Besian school massacre
(344 dead in Chechnya, teachers and children)
    transparent backdrop to this university production,
inescapable even though we close our eyes
    in the dark sometimes to wait it out, to breathe,
the convergences so fast we can barely swim
    before the swell peaks and breaks over us

preparing for another wave, another scene,
    something else we want to know, or have to, or wish we didn't,
as Washington anticipates the next strategic move
    of the Expos franchise from Montreal
and Attorney General Ashcroft prepares his resignation.
    These are days in full flight, it's true,
with early winter flowers a toxic cloying
    we can't rinse away or swallow,
while the unfledged boy on stage
    nests under every wind that blows.

Proud parents? Naturally. Our exercise,
    our mirth, our matter, you made
July's day short as December, and even some of
    Shakespeare's speech our own.
                        What was the source, then,
of my uneasiness, the finger pressing my nape. . . .
                        How well you played
the son of another, and how happy in your play, taunting royalty
    and poking them like pears grown soft.
"I am like you, they say," you say, but not
    to me, already here, colorless
in the dark, without existence, the contract of our viewing.
    "You'll kiss me hard and speak to me, as if
I were a baby still." And we would, we will,
    except we belong to another world,
driven by like-circumstance, arrivals
    unforeseen, bonds undone that we could never explicate—
still, we have a role, the reason that the play takes place: because
    we want to see it. But like lines not written, or those written over,
you can't imagine us, we're shadows of a motion

no longer going on, not part of events
folding over you, escorted in act 2 to the margin where you disappear,
     leaving us to live through the play without you, somewhere
behind the scene, the other side. . . .

And after your bows, then final bows, returned to the lit up world
and relieved by our release, we shake hands with director, cast, and
     especially your father, *your king,*
himself mostly boy for another year or two,
     scruffy, willow-lanky, his smile from
the sun, his laugh equal shade. The paternal eclipse
     he'd made as easy for him
as it was unknown, drew far past the drama, and I stared
     straight into it, to know it better
or go blind. I knew him like you know the second chime
     a bell makes—he had that power
even in silence, of possession, readiness, command,
     and I understood what he gave me to understand.

I was being charmed, though, in another way as well,
     branching in directions I couldn't see before
even as new buds popped out, drawing from present ground
     my own sapling days of insects, mold, and every kind of weather —
a synthesis of mind & world, the fusion
     of confusion with a constant light I wasn't looking for.

And I felt again something I'd missed, the ringing
     force of a boy I knew back then, when boys were what we were,
and how I wished to know him
     more than I ever could, than I could even know myself,
as some of what he meant

flashed through me, his forehead's
candor, the blond hair on his arm as he whipped
    the ball to me, that was meant for me,
as you were mine once, too, to catch,
    not keep, not carry past the line. And how
you caper in your newfound poise
    leaping between nine years
and twenty, as if you could
    by will shake a tree to part its scales
and flower.
                Even now, for now,
I resign the role, you have broken from my liking,
    and I see you join the actors in their gallery, exclusive,
irresistible, who recognize and welcome you despite your younger youth
    to the romance of the elder young
drawn to themselves in their rush to knowledge,
    their flushed embodiment
of what they'll remember of what they'll forget.

ROCK CREEK

Can two loves play and prime each other
without one shining so much brighter
it absorbs the weaker one, like brother
shadowing brother, lover lover?

We watched our boys play in the stream,
the older leading from rock to rock
and needing the younger one to seem
determined, himself, to reach the bank.

And he did seem so, gripping a hand
and shouting, held in place by one
he'd never catch with his command
wait up, wait up! and *let's pretend. . . .*

Two Indians, Indian file, in search
of soapstone they'll carve into bowl or pipe;
or hunting deer, pheasant, or perch
they'll spear and cook under a beech

whose leaves are lit to a hundred hues—
green dazzling network shifting tones,
intensities, and casting on
my eye a duplicating view:

Two boys; us two. And seeing them
        without us—one of those moments when
the weave in time breaks open—
        I thought I'd fear this intimation,   ◆

withdraw in silence; for that split
        in the continuum that raced
past the comfort of known limit
        was a complicating shadowed grace.

What soothing complications, though!
        Varieties of incandescence
like shades of understanding how
        a world is made by touching you.

The poem, still unformed, uncases me
        to find you where you are, to start
again the possibility
        of rhyming us outside of art.

What's that look like? I mean, right now,
        the conversation moving out
past the trespass we allow
        defining certainty and doubt?

I was listening, or trying to—
        and trying to make a common sound,
a stream of air on which there flew
        an understanding gaining ground.

And there was more than that to see,
    for leaves lit from above became
a screen catching light's complicity
    from stream-top to under-canopy:

lines rippling across bright pages torn,
    in constant interplay,
the light of a motion in which one turn
    returns reflection day to day.

HIKMET: ÇANKIRI PRISON, 1938

A version

Today is Sunday.
Today, for the first time, they let me go out into the sun.
And I stood there I didn't move,
struck for the first time, the very first time ever:
how far away from me the sky is
                    how blue it is
                    how wide.
I sat down, in respect, in awe, I sat down on the ground,
I leaned my back against the wall.
In this moment, there were no waves to fall into;
in this moment, there was no liberty, and no wife, my wife.
There was only the earth beneath me, the sun above me, and me.
And how I am grateful, *I am happy*, to have this thing I call *my life*.

Three

CYCLOPS

And of my two eyes only one functioning more or less correctly, I misjudged the distance separating me from the other world, and often I stretched out my hand for what was beyond my reach, and often knocked against obstacles scarcely visible on the horizons. —Samuel Beckett, *Molloy*

Before the eye that sees nothing we must take heed and tremble.
—Victor Hugo, *Les Misérables*

I.

Staring from the bathroom mirror
reflection of an eye
the hole that released me—

peering into it
I'm reminded of origins
the work I have to do.

The open pit I return to,
the granite blocks emit
waves of memory
plutonic flecks of
feldspar hornblende mica quartz.

With diamond blade I cut
dimensions I alone can lift.

I shape with carbide tip
and straight strikes
to the wedge ear
splitting trimming
squaring the edges
"letting it dance"
to close the grain.

Metabolic passions break down
experience to fuel the body
concentrating on the line of stone
building it up
block by block
line by line

under the day's bright eye,
the bright eye of night

The wall reaches
from tor to tor
outcroppings of Gaia
corner points
for my enclosure—

What space inside
for wife and child
but nowhere—
I mistake tree shadow
figments of a larger eye.

The eye like a mouth,
wants to be fed.
But what it wants to see
is now outside the wall.

An open eye
of water like a lake
nucleated, it will not
admit, shut.

It dreams among bottom weeds
grown all summer
in cool water,
dormant now, without light,
stonewort, loosestrife.

Not to dilate
like an Argive shield
blessed by the goddess in battle
but accept the arrow
why won't the eye

look past the flat screen
my sky energies
and anger flashing the stubble fields

to a smoking
arbitrary zero.

Sight beyond the walls
is binocular, two things

in relation
have depth, and
love steps
lively around
the eye
in the ground.

II.

The eye
may shut
        but
the ear has
no door   cavern
voices enter
and echo
ever after

The morning wheel turns
the owl's cry
only a dream now,
and sunflower turns
tracking the day's burning

So much to look after
Hold out your hands,
feel the luxury of the sunbeams

Do you wish

        to be something
that you are not—
        shut your eye

and drop
the measure
            of distances
to see—

———

The measure of a man?
NOVEMBER 4, 2003

standing on a narrow box
            (a box of food turned on end)
naked beneath a blanket
            fashioned into a poncho
(the design elaborate
            not an army blanket)
a cement sack
                        soaked in hot sauce
cinched
over his head
                        arms outstretched
middle fingers wired—

like a showerhead dumbly gazing down
the wires mock him
their stiff haphazard lines
routing
beneath the blanket
                        (clipped to
his nuts) the fringes
reaching for the floor
            everything in place

inside the frame
                    the figure
        throws a shadow
on the two-tone cinder wall behind him
        rusted pipes running the length
that pick up vertical woven cables in the blanket
        and accent the dimension

ABDOUH HUSSAIN SAAD FALEH
        (DETAINEE #18470):

"Then he was saying
                    'which switch
        is *on* for electricity'
And he came with a loudspeaker
        and he was shouting in my ear
and then he brought   a camera
        and he took some pictures of me"

Peering
        into the camera
the director shuts
        one eye

Look and   .
        Look   again
                again—
no
gain, it
        stares back

53

details drop
in its drift   to icon

word without sentence
repeated to emptiness

the new forever stamp
for future correspondence

—like eyespot on moth wing
it flashes startled

unfolding

flits away

light glancing off

an eye of glass

III.

When my love left
I was left with her

likeness.

Bringing it close
to my face
my eye

swelled toward it

I could feel the increased curve
eager to accommodate
currents
from the periphery.

Together
we were
two eyes
converging without rivalry
or displacement
moving—
a single radiant
sweeping

over the field
of being.

In the distance
we saw children
dueling, waves
of threats
moving toward us
making home
in the spongy
labyrinth
of membrane and bone.

We enjoyed
the impact
their bodies made
inside us.

Clouds like uprooted
mountain crags
bucked past
forming deforming
giant heads cut.

Up close
a grackle
commanded
perch on
stone wall.

Cool air
skittered the pond face.

At night
the still glass surface
filled with pinprick light
crossing border
from the firmament
to provoke
our sight.

We saw the motions
and the stillnesses,
though we were opposed
points, we extended out
along trajectories
we sighted together
to find a third one,
and make   a new space.
Paradise . . .

But the day came.
At its end
the dropping sun
stared back
—its sinking accusations . . .
an ember of the world burning
with concentrated
rapid change. And it

included us.

Hot wind
hit the eye
stole our tears.

We yellowed
conjugated
by bile.

Words lost shape in the widening crevasse.

The shadow play of futures
projected
in collaboration
vanished
on the other side
of a crooked
doorway
I couldn't pass through.
I lived alone,
my collapsing room of continual night

squinting into a framed
brightness beyond

the close dark's
comprehension.

From this far away
everything outside
looked like teeth.

One self
only
I stare
at where   she was

and see her
disappear
into the blind spot. My love
is now my love
object. Broken jar
less precious
more cherished
reassembled, freshly
frail.

I must step
over her (how?)
to make a place
for her to enter
the mind's
perpetual register.

Like a new
lock it
sticks; or a garment
once removed
too new
to hold
the body's shape.

A cataract of mist blurs the ridgeline,
birch sentinels stand with intent
waiting for a wind.

Faith in the past
dismissed without
inauguration of the present,
can there be
a new
grammar?

New habits of
cohesion
to learn, to obey new
laws of the threshold.

IV.

I had assembled
so much
paper.

The marks made long ago
accumulated
secret meanings.

Gathering hints
scattered among pages
I deciphered what I felt
mattered
and built

evidence.

When would I present my findings?

Each morning
when my eye
opened
I could feel something
resting on my
eyelid—

fluttering to dislodge it
the world slowed in strobe effect
though something
stayed there.

I was trapped
in the bracketed space
after you've raised your hand
but before you think
the answer.

When I lifted stone
on top of stone
the muscovite
winked
routed by tourmaline.

However hard the staring
no mystery flew out.

I felt their weight
and saw how they fit.
Measuring by eye
I cut blocks
precisely
no mortar needed.

Cottage-sized, each
locked into place.

Working with stone
I tried to feel the kindness of stone
what perfect strength it must hold
to be a wall.

But scanning for gaps
between stones
fissures   misalignments
parentheses of weakness
I was the teacher
whose students learned
something about him
he had not learned himself
standing before them
morning after morning

Feasting day came,
I had no appetite
but to see
                my pages

burn.

Moonless
eyeless night.

Carting it all
just outside the wall

I soon
watched flames
cast on stone
a new kind of shadow play.

I introduced them
once so coddled
one by one
to the elemental dance of the forge
relishing the crackling
shriveling films
and floating ash.

Some
lifting high
I could still track
carried by the night tide.

As if consumed myself
I wanted to grasp the flame!
—to receive nothing
but its warmth
was a poverty . . .
(What would change
permanently

the cells of the body?)

Growing hungry
I roasted an egg there
blackening zero in the embers

and when I cracked it
pulled apart the white
the cooked yolk
stared back   birth pit
hard yellow germ
sun seed.

Conceiving what I cannot
know, knowing
what I do not yet
understand, I can only try
to make preparations
for the necessary valor.

The eye must shut
to become a stone of perfect kindness
to let seeds

shoot up with impersonal needs
for the first time
opening.

NOTES

Sources for "Rock Creek (II)" include Philip Ball's *Flow: Nature's Patterns: A Tapestry in Three Parts* (New York: Oxford University Press, 2009); Fergus Bordewich's *Washington: The Making of the American Capital* (New York: Amistad, 2008); Steve Dryden's *Peirce Mill: Two Hundred Years in the Nation's Capital* (Washington, DC: Bergamot, 2009); William Bushong's historical resource study, *Rock Creek Park, District of Columbia* (Ann Arbor: University of Michigan Library, 1990); Walt Whitman's *Specimen Days* (New York: Library of America, 1996); *Walt Whitman's Civil War* (New York: Da Capo, 1989); Scott Higham and Sari Horwitz's *Finding Chandra: A True Washington Murder Mystery* (New York: Scribner, 2010); Pradeep K. Behera et al., *Wet Weather Flow Characterization for the Rock Creek through Monitoring and Modeling*, prepared for the DC Water Resources Research Institute (Washington, DC, 2007); *Our Hero Handbook: A Guide for Families of Wounded Soldiers* (Carlisle, PA: US Army War College, 2006). The "ex-con/activist" is Ralph Waldo "Petey" Green. "The Poet of the Sierras" a.k.a. "The Kit Carson of Poetry" is Joaquin Miller, author of "Columbus." The poet who suffered my trespass with forbearance and in friendship is John Fitzpatrick.

"The Figure of a Man Being Swallowed by a Fish" responds to an anonymous and eponymous folk sculpture in the permanent collection of the Baltimore Museum of Art. A recording of the poem is part of the museum's "60 Objects" audio tour.

"Things To Do While You're Here" is for Jonathan Rosen.

"The Winter's Tale" was written following the staging of Shakespeare's play at George Washington University, October 26–29, 2005, directed by Alan Wade. The poem is addressed to my son, but he shares its dedication with Robert Pinsky.

"Hikmet: Çankiri Prison, 1938" is for Murat Tarimcilar, who introduced me to the poem and provided the literal translation from the Turkish, upon which this imitation is based.

"Cyclops II" is indebted to Mark Danner's *Torture and Truth: America, Abu Ghraib, and the War on Terror* (New York: New York Review of Books, 2004) and *Standard Operating Procedure*, a film by Errol Morris (2008).